Standard Bible Story Readers

BOOK FOUR
(THE THIRD READER)

BY
LILLIE A. FARIS
First Grade Critic Teacher, College of Education of
Ohio University, Athens, O.

Illustrated by O. A. STEMLER and BESS BRUCE CLEVELAND

———————— ✣ ————————

THE STANDARD PUBLISHING COMPANY
CINCINNATI, O.

Printed in U. S. A.

GRATEFUL ACKNOWLEDGMENT

As the fourth book in the series of Standard Bible Story Readers comes
from the press the author feels more deeply than ever before her
sense of gratitude to the boys and girls who have expressed their
enjoyment in the reading of the earlier books of the series;
to the teachers and educators who have so enthusiasti-
cally endorsed their content; to the publishers and
their force of skilled artists who have labored
willingly to make the mechanical workman-
ship of the highest type, and to all who
have lent their sympathetic interest
to the publication of the series.

CONTENTS

FAIREST LORD JESUS

Fairest Lord Jesus,
King of creation;
O Thou of God and man the Son!
Truly I'll love Thee,
Truly I'll serve Thee,
Light of my soul, my Joy, my Crown.

Fair are the meadows,
Fairer the woodlands,
Robed in the blooming garb of spring;
Jesus is fairer,
Jesus is purer,
He makes our sorrowing spirits sing.

Fair is the sunshine,
Fairer the moonlight,
And all the twinkling starry hosts;
Jesus shines brighter,
Jesus shines purer,
Than all the angels heaven can boast.

—Silesian Folk Song.

7

A GRAND OLD HERO

Nearly two thousand years before Christ was born there lived a wonderful old man whose name was Abraham. Abraham was true to God and always tried to do what was right, but many of the people who lived in his country did not care to please God.

One day God spoke to Abraham and said: "Get thee out of thy country and from thy kindred and from thy father's house into a land that I will show thee, and I will make of thee a great nation." It was a wonderful promise to come to any one, and, of course, Abraham was willing to do what God had asked of him. He did not ask where he was to go, but simply trusted God's word and knew that everything would be all right.

8

Abraham took his wife, whose name was
Sarah, and his nephew, Lot, and his family. And they, with their flocks and herds,
and the servants who tended these flocks
and herds, started to go just where they
were directed. They journeyed on until
they came to a land called Canaan, and
when they reached that land God spoke
to Abraham, saying: "This is the land
which I give to you." And Abraham
builded an altar and thanked God for
His goodness.

In the days when Abraham lived the people
wore long-flowing robes and usually had
cloth turbans over their heads; the women
wove the cloth out of which these things
were made. The cloth was made from the
wool of the sheep, or from camel's hair.
The houses were made of cloth, too, and

when the people moved from one place to another they rolled up their tents, or homes, and carried them with them.

Once when Abraham and his people lived in the land of Canaan which God had given them, a great famine swept over the land and they had to hunt for a better place, where they might find food for their flocks.

They went into the land of Egypt, and there was plenty of pasture and water there. They stayed there for some time, and then planned to return to the land which God had given to Abraham.

Abraham was seventy-five years old when God spoke to him the first time, and when he was almost a hundred God appeared to him again. He made the same wonderful promise to Abraham, that he should be the father of a great nation. A little later Abraham was sitting by his tent door under some great oak-trees, and he lifted up his eyes and saw three angels standing there.

These angels had come to bring him a message, and the good, old man was very kind to them. He sent his servants to bring water to wash their feet. Then he called to his wife, saying: "Oh, Sarah, there are some strangers here—three of them—and we must get them some lunch right away. Get some fine meal and knead it and make the cakes upon the hearth."

Abraham himself went out and found a young, tender calf, and had it dressed just as quickly as possible; then he brought some milk and butter, and they had lunch out under the tree.

The angels told Abraham that it would not be long before a little son should be born in his family, and this promise came true.

When Abraham was one hundred years old, Isaac was born, and the home was very happy.

Perhaps one of the hardest trials that ever came to any man came to Abraham when Isaac had grown up to be quite a fine, sturdy lad. One day God said: "Now, Abraham, take thy son Isaac and go up into the land of Moriah, and offer him there as a burnt-offering upon one of the mountains which I shall tell thee of."

It was not the nature of this grand old man to question anything that God asked of him. And this time, even though he was sorely grieved, he did not doubt but that everything would work out just right.

Very early the next morning he and his young
son, Isaac, and two servants, started to
go to the country of which God had spoken.
On the third day they came to the place.
Abraham asked the young men to wait for
him while he and Isaac went on a little
farther. Then he stopped to build the
altar on which his son Isaac was to be
offered.

He placed the wood for the offering, took the
knife in his hand, and Isaac looked at him
and said: "My father, behold the fire and
the wood, but where is the lamb for the
burnt-offering?" In Abraham's answer
you will see just how much he trusted
God. He said: "My son, God will provide
himself with a lamb for the offering."

It must have been very hard for Abraham
when Isaac asked this question of him.

16

He finished fixing the wood and had the
fire all ready, then he bound Isaac and laid
him upon the altar.

The old man took the knife in his hand, and
just as he lifted it an angel spoke from
the very gate of heaven and said: "Abraham, lay not thy hand upon the lad.
Neither do thou anything to him, for now
I know thou fearest God, seeing thou hast
not withheld thy son, thine only son, from
me."

Just then Abraham looked and saw a ram
caught by his horns in the thicket, and he
took the ram and offered it instead of his
son Isaac.

God only wanted to test Abraham's faith in
Him, and Abraham had been willing to do
anything for God, even to the giving his
only son as a sacrifice.

ISAAC

After Isaac had grown to manhood, he married
a very beautiful woman, whose name was
Rebekah. He lived in the land of Canaan, and, after a few years, a famine
came.

He and his family started to go to the land of
Egypt, but God appeared unto him and
said: "Go not down into Egypt; dwell in
the land that I shall tell thee of, and I
will be with thee and bless thee." Then
Isaac and his family lived in the land
of which God told him. It was a place
called Gerar.

Every bit of seed that Isaac sowed grew; his
flocks increased greatly, and everything
came to pass just as God said it would.
He had many servants, and all of them

were kept busy attending to his great flocks of sheep and herds of cattle.

In the days when his father, Abraham, had lived, many wells had been digged by Abraham's herdsmen; these had later been filled up by an enemy. Isaac needed the water for his flocks, and he put his servants to cleaning out the wells. Just as soon as Isaac's herdsmen would clean a well and the water would come bubbling forth, the people who lived in that country would claim the well. They said, "That water is ours."

Isaac's servants might have disputed with these men about the well, but their master said to them, "Dig another." He did not wish to quarrel with any one. The servants digged another well, and these same people came and claimed it, too.

Perhaps it would seem this time that Isaac's men should claim the water and fight these people off, but that was not his way; he just asked his herdsmen to dig another well, and then those people that lived in the land of Gerar learned the great lesson Isaac had been teaching them; it was that a well of water is not worth fighting over, that nothing in the world is worth fighting over, and that, even though one feels that he has been wronged, it always takes two sides to make a quarrel.

JOSEPH

Jacob was a man who had twelve sons, but there was none so well known as Joseph. Joseph had always been a good lad. He used to like to sit beside his grandfather, Isaac, and hear the stories which the old man would tell. Perhaps Isaac told him of the day when his own father, Abraham, had taken him up to the mountain to offer him as a sacrifice to God, and how, just when his father's hand was lifted to strike, God's voice had spoken from heaven telling him not to do that thing. Joseph loved the part of the story that told about God's voice coming down from heaven, and how Abraham had looked around and found a ram caught in the bushes, and he had used it for the sacrifice.

When the older brothers of Joseph were out watching the flocks, no doubt he had many good times with his grandfather. Perhaps some of these stories helped him to be a fine, strong lad.

You remember how Joseph's brothers put him down in the dark pit, and the traders came along the road and bought him so that they might sell him as a slave in the land of Egypt.

When he reached the country of Egypt he was sold to a man whose name was Potiphar, and he had charge of Potiphar's household. He managed all of Potiphar's servants; here is where Joseph proved himself a very great hero. One day Potiphar's wife wanted him to do something very wrong, and Joseph refused. The woman was so angry that when her husband came

home she told a wicked lie about Joseph. Potiphar believed what his wife had told him and ordered Joseph put in prison, but God was with him all the time and gave him great blessings. It was while Joseph was in the prison that the king of Egypt had a strange dream which nobody could explain to him, and Joseph was called. When he told the king the meaning of the dream the king was very much pleased with him and gave him a beautiful chariot in which to ride, and ordered that he should be dressed in the very finest clothing. And Joseph worked for the king many years. He may have wondered why his old father never tried to find him, for he did not know that the wicked brothers had made their father believe that some wild beast had torn him to pieces; but after many years his brothers were forced to go to the land of Egypt to get some food for their families, and again Joseph proved himself a real hero.

He had the power to put his brothers in prison. He could have caused them a great deal of trouble; he might even have taken their lives if he had wished to do so, but he was not that kind of a man. Down in his heart he was just planning how he could get them all to come over to his land, where they might always have food and be happy.

Joseph's kind heart would not let him punish his brothers; he would not even take any pay for the corn which they had bought. When they got home each one found his money in the sack. He had told them, however, that when they came back if they did not bring their youngest brother, Benjamin, he would not let them have the corn. He had told them also if they were true men they would allow one of the brothers to stay there as a surety that they would come again.

It had been a very hard matter for Joseph to keep his secret; he almost felt that he would have to tell them that he was Joseph, but he did not.

The second time the brothers had to go to Joseph for corn they knew that they would have to take Benjamin, and they had a very hard time getting the father to understand that Benjamin should go. Poor old Jacob was so afraid he would lose Benjamin as he had Joseph. At last, however, he told them that Benjamin might go with them.

This time Joseph planned that he would keep Benjamin there with him in order to get his father to come. He had one of his servants slip a silver cup into Benjamin's sack, and then after the men had started home he told the servants to go after them and bring back the one in whose sack they found the silver cup. When they found this was Benjamin, the brothers felt very sad. They did not know how they could go home and leave Benjamin there. They said, "It will kill our father." They went back to Joseph and begged him to let Benjamin go back with them. One of them said: "Our father's life is bound up in the lad, and when he sees that the lad is not with us he will die, and I promised that when I returned Benjamin should be with me."

29

"Then Judah came near unto him, and said,
Oh, my lord, let thy servant, I pray thee,
speak a word in my lord's ears, and let not
thine anger burn against thy servant; for
thou art even as Pharaoh.

My lord asked his servants, saying, Have ye
a father, or a brother?

And we said unto my lord, We have a father,
an old man, and a child of his old age, a
little one; and his brother is dead, and he
alone is left of his mother; and his father
loveth him.

And thou saidst unto thy servants, Bring him
down unto me, that I may set mine eyes
upon him.

And we said unto my lord, The lad cannot
leave his father: for if he should leave
his father, his father would die.

And thou saidst unto thy servants, Except

your youngest brother come down with you, ye shall see my face no more.

And it came to pass when we came up unto thy servant, my father, we told him the words of my lord.

And our father said, Go again, buy us a little food.

And we said, We cannot go down: if our youngest brother be with us, then will we go down; for we may not see the man's face, except our youngest brother be with us.

And thy servant, my father, said unto us, Ye know that my wife bare me two sons:

And the one went out from me, and I said, Surely he is torn in pieces; and I have not seen him since:

And if ye take this one also from me, and harm befall him, ye will bring down my gray hairs with sorrow to Sheol.

Now therefore, when I come to thy servant my
father, and the lad is not with us; seeing
that his life is bound up in the lad's life;
It will come to pass, when he seeth that the
lad is not with us, that he will die: and
thy servants will bring down the gray
hairs of thy servant, our father, with sorrow to Sheol.
For thy servant became surety for the lad unto
my father, saying, If I bring him not unto
thee, then shall I bear the blame to my
father for ever.
Now, therefore, let thy servant, I pray thee,
abide instead of the lad a bondman to my
lord; and let the lad go up with his
brethren.
For how shall I go up to my father, if the lad
be not with me? lest I see the evil that
shall come on my father."

Joseph sent everybody but his brothers from the room. Then he wept aloud and said to them: "I am Joseph. Doth my father yet live?" The brothers fell down on their knees before him, for they were so ashamed and grieved, but Joseph said to them: "It was God's way to send me here to save you all from the great famine. Go up to my father and tell him that I am yet alive. Tell my father of all the glory in Egypt and of all that you have seen, and bring my father hither." Then Joseph kissed all his brethren and wept with them.

There was much excitement in the castle when Pharaoh heard that Joseph's brethren were there, and he was so pleased he gave them great, wonderful presents to carry home to their father. He told them to bring their father and come back and live in his country. He said: "I will give you the good of the land of Egypt, and ye shall eat the fat of the land. Take wagons out of the land of Egypt for your little ones and for your wives, and bring your father and come, for the good of all the land of Egypt is yours."

When the brothers went home and told their old father that Joseph was alive, he said: "It is enough; Joseph, my son, is yet alive: I will go and see him before I die."

Just as soon as they could get things ready they all started for Egypt, and Jacob was very happy indeed when he saw his beloved son Joseph.

Jacob was very happy to spend the rest of his life in Egypt, and Joseph's family treated him in the kindest way.

A PSALM

Make a joyful noise unto
Jehovah, all ye lands.
Serve Jehovah with gladness:
Come before His presence with
singing.
Know ye that Jehovah, He is God:
It is He that hath made us, and
we are His.
We are His people, and the sheep
of His pasture.
Enter into His gates with thanks-
giving,
And into His courts with praise.
Give thanks unto Him, and bless
His name.
For Jehovah is good: His lovingkindness
endureth for ever,
And His faithfulness unto all generations.

—Psalm 100.

ONLY ONE MOTHER

Imogene Humphrey.

1. Hundreds of stars in the pret-ty sky, Hundreds of shells on the
2. Hundreds of birds that go wing-ing by, Hundreds of bees in the

shore to-geth-er.
sun-ny weath-er. 3. Hundreds of dew-drops to greet the dawn,

Hundreds of lambs in the pur-ple clo-ver. 4. Hundreds of but-ter-flies

on the lawn, But on-ly one moth-er the wide world o-ver.

MOSES

Moses was one of the greatest heroes that ever
lived in any age of the world. Everybody
remembers the story of the little Hebrew
boy who was put in the basket boat and
placed where the Pharaoh's daughter
would be sure to find him. Everybody
remembers how the Pharaoh's daughter
named him Moses because she drew him
out of the water, and then how she sent
for the baby's own mother to nurse and
care for him. That part of the story is
well known to almost every boy and girl.
A great many things entered into the life of
this boy to make him a hero. When he
was old enough to go to the king's palace to live, he was taken there, and the
princess loved and cared for him as
though he were her own son.

The princess wanted Moses to have the very
best teachers, so that he could fill the rank
of a prince in the finest way. Everything
that was necessary to make his life happy
was given to him in the palace, and Moses
lived there for about forty years.

In some way he came to know that he was not
an Egyptian, but that he belonged to the
Hebrew people. The people of Egypt were
not very kind to the Hebrews; they beat
and lashed the Hebrews and made them
work like slaves.

One day when Moses was walking out he saw
an Egyptian beating one of the Hebrews,
and it made him very angry. He could
not stand it to see his people treated in
that sort of way, and he killed the
Egyptian. Moses knew that he would
not dare stay in the country of Egypt

longer, and he went away to the land of Midian for safety.

He wandered about in this land for some time, and one day sat down by a well. While he was sitting there seven young women who were taking care of their father's sheep came over to the well to water their flocks. Some shepherds came and tried to drive the young women away, so that they might water their own flocks first, but Moses stood up and helped the young women. He kept the shepherds back and drew the water for the women. When the girls' father learned that Moses had helped them, he said to them: "Why did you leave him? Why didn't you call him to come and eat with us?" Then Moses was invited to the man's home, and stayed there for a long time.

Moses was about forty years old when he went to the land of Midian, and he stayed in that land for forty years. He had become a shepherd and cared for the flocks of a man whose name was Jethro. Moses had married one of the young women for whom he had drawn the water.

One day as Moses was keeping the flock of his father-in-law, Jethro, he came to a mountain called Mt. Horeb. It was here that a very great test came to Moses. All at once he saw a flame of fire coming out from the midst of a bush, and as he looked, behold, the bush burned with fire, and it was not consumed. Moses wondered why the bush was not burned up, and, suddenly, right from the midst of the bush a voice said, "Moses, Moses." Moses answered, "Here am I." And God's voice

spoke again: "Put off thy shoes from off thy feet, for the place whereon thou standest is holy ground."

Moses was astonished, but he did as God commanded, and he received a most wonderful message. He was called to be the leader of the people of Israel.

Could he return to that land? He had already refused wealth and honor, and had turned away because he could not stand it to see his people abused. That had been a hard thing, and he had killed a man over there! Now, would he dare return?

But Moses did not hesitate long. He hid his face as God talked to him, and the Voice said: "Come thou therefore, and I will send thee unto Pharaoh, that thou mayest bring forth my people, the children of Israel, out of Egypt."

Moses was not sure that he could do what God had asked. He knew that he was willing, but he feared to undertake such a great work. But when the promise came from God, "Certainly I will be with thee," he did not hesitate longer.

Then there were some great messages to Moses, telling him just how he should go and what he should do; how he should call the officers of the people of Israel together, and how he should go before the Pharaoh.

After Moses had listened to all that God wanted to tell him, he returned to Jethro's house and talked the matter over with him. Jethro said to Moses, "Go in peace."

Then there was a wonderful time in Egypt when Moses went and called the elders together as he had been told; there were directions to be given; there were all sorts of plans for the long journey back to their home country; there were little children to be taken care of, and there were some older people to be cared for also; and then, hardest of all, it took a long time to get the king's permission for them to go. At a certain time all the thousands of people of Israel were to start on the long, long journey away from the land of Egypt back to their old home in Canaan. God's plan was that in the daytime they should be guided by a white cloud, and at night by a pillar of fire. He had told Moses that whenever the cloud stopped they should stop, and whenever it moved on they should move on, and you may know that they were guided exactly right.

Many times they were discouraged, and they found much fault with their leader, but God was always with him.

It was on this long journey, one day at Mount Sinai, that God gave Moses the Ten Commandments, which you know so well.

It took about forty years of wandering before these people reached the promised land, and then one day God took Moses up on a great, high mountain called Nebo, and showed him all the country that stretched away to the west—that country was the land of Canaan.

Moses was now one hundred and twenty years old, and God saw that it was time for him to rest from his labors. He showed him the beautiful country and then honored him in the finest way that any one ever was honored. The beautiful poem, which follows, tells about Moses' burial:

By Nebo's lonely mountain,
    On this side Jordan's wave,
In a vale in the land of Moab,
    There lies a lonely grave.
But no man knows that sepulchre,
    And no man saw it e'er;
For the angels of God upturned the sod
    And laid the dead man there.

That was the grandest funeral
    That ever passed on earth;
But no man heard the trampling,
    Or saw the train go forth.
Noiselessly as the daylight comes
    When the night is done,
And the crimson streak on ocean's cheek
    Grows into the great sun;

Noiselessly as the springtime
    Her crest of verdure weaves,
And all the trees on all the hills
    Open their thousand leaves—

So, without sound of music,
  Or voice of them that wept,
Silently down from the mountain crown
  The great procession swept.

This was the bravest warrior
  That ever buckled sword;
This the most gifted poet
  That ever breathed a word;
And never earth's philosopher
  Traced, with his golden pen,
On the deathless page, truths half so sage
  As he wrote down for men.

And had he not high honor?
  The hillside for his pall;
To lie in state while angels wait
  With the stars for tapers tall;
And the dark rock pines, like tossing plumes,
  Over his bier to wave;
And God's own hand, in that lonely land,
  To lay him in his grave.

—*Cecil Frances Alexander.*

GOD'S LOVE

He prayeth well, who loveth well
　　Both man and bird and beast;
He prayeth best, who loveth best
　　All things, both great and small.
For the dear God, who loveth us,
　　He made and loveth all.

—Samuel Coleridge.

RUTH, THE TRUE-HEARTED

Mahlon and Chilion were two Jewish boys who lived with their father and mother in a little town not far from Jerusalem. Their mother was a very lovely woman, whose name was Naomi, and their father's name was Elimelech.

Sometimes a famine would sweep over the land, and people who did not have great stores of food were forced to go into a different country to get the things which they needed.

During one of these famines Elimelech and Naomi took their boys and moved into the land of Moab, where there was plenty of food.

Everything was very strange to them in the land of Moab, but the people were kind and good, and they soon had a new home. They had plenty to eat, and everything went well with them for a time, but the father grew sick, and at last died, leaving his wife, Naomi, and the two boys, who were fast growing up.

After Mahlon and Chilion had grown to be young men, they told their mother about two beautiful girls in the land of Moab whom they would like to bring to her home to be her daughters. Naomi wanted her boys to be happy, and she told them to marry the girls and bring them home, and they would all share the home together.

At last, one day, two daughters, whose names were Orpah and Ruth, came to live with Naomi, and they were very kind and helpful to her, making the little home as bright as could possibly be.

After a time another great sadness came. Both the boys became ill and died, leaving Naomi and Orpah and Ruth in the little home together. Naomi was so very sad that she determined she would go back home to Bethlehem among her old neighbors and friends. Good news had come about the old home: the rains had come and there was plenty of barley and wheat and other food. This made Naomi want to go more than ever.

Orpah and Ruth helped Naomi get ready to go back. There was not very much for her to take with her, and the girls started down the road to go part of the way so that she would not feel so lonesome. They loved her very much, and yet they knew that it would be better for her to go back home.

At last, after they had walked a long way, Naomi kissed the girls good-by and told them to go back among their own people, where they would be happy. The girls threw their arms around Naomi and cried, because they felt they would never see her again. They begged to stay with her, but she told them they would be happier among their own people, and she begged them to go back to their homes. At last, Orpah kissed her mother and started back, but Ruth clung to Naomi and said: "Entreat me not to leave thee, and to return from following after thee; for whither thou goest, I will go; and where thou lodgest, I will lodge; thy people shall be my people, and thy God my God; where thou diest will I die, and there will I be buried."

When Naomi saw how very much Ruth loved
her and wanted to go to Bethlehem with
her, she felt less lonely, and the two
walked side by side until they reached
the little town.

As they came up to Bethlehem the old neighbors and friends of Naomi were very
busy in the barley-fields, which were full
of waving, heavy grain. Many of the
friends paused to greet Naomi as she
came back to the old town, and she told
them of the sadness which had come into
her life.

The friends were sorry for her, but they were
also glad to greet the new, beautiful
daughter-in-law that had come back with
her. And would you like to know how
Ruth liked the new people?

This is what she did: she went right out in

58

the barley-fields that belonged to some rich men and began to gather from the ground the grain which the reapers dropped, so that her mother-in-law, Na-omi, might have food.

The men did not have great machines such as we have to reap the grain, but they carried long knives and piled the grain up on their arms. Some of it would fall down, and then any one who wanted it was welcome to pick it up.

Ruth gathered great armfuls of the barley as the people let it fall, and carried it home.

One day when she was hard at work the man who owned the fields saw her. He did not know who she was, but he asked the man who had charge of the work, and the man said: "That is the young woman

who came from the land of Moab with
Naomi. She has been working hard."

The rich man, whose name was Boaz, watched
Ruth. He thought she must be very
kind-hearted to do all that for Naomi,
and he gave orders that his servants
should let more grain fall than was really
necessary, so that she might have a
great deal.

Ruth knew that Boaz was unusually kind to
her; she went to him and bowed before
him. She said: "Why are you so kind to
me, since I am a stranger?"

And Boaz answered: "I have been told all
that you have done for Naomi since she
has had so much sadness. I have heard
how you left your father and mother and
homeland and have come to this strange
country. May God repay you for your

work and reward you, for you have taken refuge under his wings."

Ruth gleaned all day, and after she had rubbed out all the barley grains, she found that she had almost a bushel.

She was so happy when she went home to her mother-in-law because she had been able to get so much food.

Naomi was very happy too. Ruth told her all about Boaz and his kindness. Then Naomi told Ruth that Boaz was their kinsman, and that she was glad he had been so kind.

Ruth was true to the word which she gave to Naomi that day when she said: "Where thou goest, I will go; where thou lodgest, I will lodge; thy people shall be my people, and thy God my God," and she became a wonderful helper in God's work.

KIND HEARTS

Longfellow.

Lillien L. Helburn.

1. Kind hearts are the gar- dens, Kind thoughts are the roots,
2. Take care of the gar- dens, And keep them from weeds,

Kind words are the flow - ers, Kind deeds are the fruits.
Fill, fill them with flow - ers, Kind words and kind deeds.

"I would be true,
   For there are those who love me."

GIDEON

It must have been a very strange thing to see an angel come from heaven and sit under a great oak-tree, but that is just the thing that happened one time when a young man, not very far away, was working on the threshing-floor. The young man's name was Gideon, and he was going to hide the wheat away just as soon as it was all threshed out.

Of course, this story happened in the long-ago time when people had to thresh their wheat in a very strange, slow way. The wheat stalks were piled together and the wheat seeds were beaten out of their hulls, then the chaff was blown away and the wheat gathered into vessels.

As the young man was working away the angel appeared and said to him, "Jeho-

vah is with thee, thou mighty man of
valor."

Gideon stopped to think of the things that
had been happening to his people, and
he wondered how it could be if God were
with them that their enemies were de-
stroying everything which they pos-
sessed, and he answered: "Jehovah has
cast us off. Our fathers used to tell us
that He brought us out of the land of
Egypt, but He has surely forsaken us."

Then a great command came to Gideon from
God: "Go in thy might and save Israel
from the hands of the enemy. Have I
not sent thee?"

The poor man, Gideon, looked at the angel
and said: "How can I save Israel? Look
at me. I am from the poorest family,
and I am the least in my father's house."

Gideon was not quite sure who it was talking to him. He thought it was a voice from God, but he said: "Show me a sign that it is really God that is talking to me. Stay here until I go get my present." And the angel who was bringing God's message answered: "I will tarry until thou come again."

Then Gideon went and got the present ready. He took a little goat and some meal and put the flesh in a basket and put the broth in a pot, and took it out under the oak-tree and gave it to the angel.

The angel said: "You take the flesh and the cakes, and put them on this rock and pour the broth over them."

After Gideon had done this the angel took the staff which he carried in his hand and touched the flesh with it, and it was

burned up immediately. Then the angel
disappeared, and Gideon knew that he
had truly carried God's message.

After awhile all the enemies of God's people
gathered themselves together to fight,
and Gideon went out by himself to talk
to God about it. He said: "O Jehovah,
I will put a fleece of wool on the threshing-floor; and if there be dew on the
fleece and the ground all be dry, then I
will know that Thou wilt save Israel by
my hand."

Then Gideon put the fleece of wool out, and
very early in the morning went and
picked it up, and the dew had fallen on
it so heavily that he wrung out a whole
bowl full of water.

Gideon was so afraid that he would make
some mistake, he said: "O Lord, do not

be angry with me, let me try once more; to-night let me put the fleece out, and if Thou wilt be with me let the fleece be dry and let the ground be covered with dew."

And the next morning when he went to get the fleece it was dry and the ground was all wet with dew. Then Gideon was just sure that God would be with him.

Gideon called a great army of thirty-two thousand people together, and they camped by a spring. There was a stream of water flowing from the spring. Far to the north of them was the camp of the Midianites; there were many thousands of them, too, and Gideon's task was a very great one.

God saw Gideon's army and knew that His power would be far greater if He did not use so many men. He said to Gideon: "You have too many men. Tell them if there is any one afraid he may go back home."

Gideon spoke to the men and gave them God's message. "If any of you are afraid, you may return to your homes." And twenty-two thousand of the men turned and went to their homes. Ten thousand only were left.

God wanted the children of Israel to understand that He was helping them, and He said to Gideon: "The people are yet too many. Bring them down by the water and I will try them for thee."

Gideon took all the men down to the water. The men were to be tested in a very strange way. God told Gideon to have all the men take a drink of water; then

He watched them drink. He said: "Gideon, put all the men that lap water like a dog in one place, and put all those that get down on their knees to drink in another place."

There were three hundred of the ten thousand that stooped and dipped up the water in their hands and drank as they went along. All the rest of them waited to get down on their knees to drink.

God was pleased with the three hundred men who drank as they went along, and He said to Gideon: "I will save your army and give the Midianites into your hand by these three hundred men."

All the rest of the men were sent to their tents, and the three hundred whom God had chosen waited for their orders from Gideon.

That very night God appeared to Gideon
and told him that he should go over into
the camp of the enemy and listen to
what they were saying. God said: "If
you fear to go, take some one with you."
Gideon went, and this is what he heard.
One man said: "I have had a dream. I
dreamed that a cake of barley bread
came tumbling into the camp and into
the tent and struck the tent so hard that
it fell and lay flat." And the man who
was listening said: "Well, that means
that the sword of Gideon shall overcome
all our hosts of people."
Then Gideon went back to the camp of Israel
and told the three hundred men who
were to go with him, to arise and make
ready. He divided the men into com-
panies of one hundred each. He gave

each of them a trumpet and an empty pitcher with a torch on the inside of it. Then he told them to watch very carefully what he did, and for each of them to do exactly the thing that he did. He said: "When I blow the trumpet you will do the same on every side of the camp and all cry out, 'For the Lord and for Gideon.' "

It was just about ten o'clock at night when Gideon and his men surrounded the camp of the enemy. New men were on watch around the camp. When Gideon blew his trumpet all the men blew their trumpets; they broke the pitchers and held aloft the torches in their left hands and their trumpets in their right hands, and cried out: "The sword of the Lord and of Gideon."

The Midianites were so frightened they could not see that there were only a few men after them; they thought there were thousands upon thousands attacking them, and they fled in terror. Then it was easy for the children of Israel to seize the country and to stop the trouble which the Midianites were giving them.

GOD'S GOODNESS

Elizabeth Jenkins.

Lillien E. Landman.

1. How glad I am God made for me, The beau - ty
2. How won - der - ful it is to dwell, In this big

of a rust - ling tree, The love - ly rose whose leaves un-
world He made so well, The Lord just told it all to

fold, And let me see her heart of gold.
be, And that it was for you and me.

75

JONATHAN

The people of Israel, although they were
God's chosen people, did not always do
the things which He had asked of them.
They would try for a little while, then
something would happen which would
make them forget all about God and His
goodness to them.

So many times these people grumbled and
complained; they complained against
their great leaders and against God,
and sometimes it was necessary for them
to be punished for their wrong-doing.

They had a great deal of trouble with some
heathen people. The people of Israel
had never had a king. God had tried to
teach them to take care of themselves,
but they had grumbled and complained.

God had sent judges to rule over them, but the people clamored and cried for a king. Finally, God gave them their wish, and a young man whose name was Saul was chosen as the first king.

Saul was the king of Israel for a good many years, and during his reign there was a heathen king who gave him a lot of trouble. The heathen people were called Philistines, and they were very large and powerful.

They gave King Saul no end of trouble; when they saw that he was king they decided they would make his life a sorry one, and they would come along the borders and steal the things that the children of Israel had, and finally many of King Saul's people were so frightened that they hid themselves.

At last King Saul became tired of the things
these people were doing, and he raised
an army of men to attack the Philistines
whenever they caused more trouble. He
put some of these men high up on the
mountainsides. The king had a son,
Prince Jonathan, who was a very fine
soldier, and he gave Jonathan command
of a thousand of his men.

The Philistines had a great army camped up
on the hillsides, and Jonathan was not
content to wait until something happened; he wanted to stir up things himself. He spoke to his armor-bearer:
"Let us go up over to the Philistines'
garrison."

Jonathan was very careful not to tell his father that he was going. The armor-
bearer was very glad to go with Jon-

athan, and the two started out. As they
went along Jonathan said: "We will go
over unto the men and tell them who we
are, and if they invite us up where they
are we will go." Jonathan said: "We
need not be afraid, for God is with us."
Finally Jonathan and his servant reached
the place, and the Philistines said, "Come
up." Both of them went up on the
mountainside. There were about twenty
men on duty for the Philistines, and
Jonathan and his armor-bearer destroyed
all of them. All the people in the camp
became frightened, and there was a
great earthquake, and the Philistines
rushed wildly in every direction.
When King Saul's soldiers saw the people
running away and disappearing, they
tried to find out what had happened.

King Saul said: "Number and see who is gone from us." And when they began to number they found out that Prince Jonathan and his armor-bearer were the ones who were gone. Then King Saul called all his soldiers together and came to battle. A lot more of the children of Israel who had been hidden in the caves in the hills came out and joined Saul's army, and soon the Philistines were driven away. Jonathan's bravery had saved his father's army.

THE PRAYER JESUS TAUGHT

Our Father which art in heaven,

Hallowed be thy name.

Thy kingdom come.

Thy will be done in earth,

as it is in heaven.

Give us this day our daily bread.

And forgive us our debts,

as we forgive our debtors.

And lead us not into temptation,

but deliver us from evil:

For thine is the kingdom,

and the power,

and the glory,

forever.

Amen.

Matt. 6: 9-13.

A CHANCE TO GET EVEN

You have heard many times the story of a
shepherd lad, whose name was David,
killing a wicked giant who tormented his
king's people. Saul was the king's name,
and David was just a shepherd boy who
tended his father's sheep on the plains of
Bethlehem.

David went to live in the king's palace so that
he might play beautiful music for the king
and keep him from the moody spells which
sometimes came upon him.

King Saul was very happy with David until
the time when the people of his kingdom
began to praise David; and when they
sang,

"Saul hath slain his thousands,
But David his ten thousands,"

it was more than King Saul could bear. He made up his mind that he would kill David. One day he threw a spear at David, but it missed him and stuck in the wall.

Then it was that Prince Jonathan helped David to get away from his father's house, and David found that it would be better for him to go away off and hide from the king. He kept hidden for several years, and one day one of the king's men happened to see him. This man went right up to the palace and told the king where David was.

King Saul called his men together, about three thousand in all, and asked them to go with him to find David and kill him. These men went very close to the place where David was hiding and pitched their tents.

David's men were watching, and he sent some
spies out to find just what King Saul
intended to do. These spies saw where
the men were camping and went back and
told David. David then went out to find
where King Saul was. He said to his men,
"Who will go with me to Saul's camp?"
There was a very brave man whose name was
Abishai, who said to David, "I will go with
you." David and Abishai went down to
Saul's camp at night, when he was sleep-
ing. King Saul's spear was stuck in the
ground at his head, and by his side there
was a cruse of water.
All the men around the king were asleep, and
Abishai said to David: "See, he is asleep;
let me take this spear and kill him."
David had such a good chance to kill the old
king who had been so ugly to him, and

who was even then trying to take his life. It was the best chance in the world, but David was not a coward; he would not slip up when any one was unaware of his coming; he had no thought of going behind the king's back and striking him when he had no chance to strike back. A hero does not do that way.

David said to Abishai: "No, you must not destroy him, because you would be guilty of striking God's chosen king. His time will come; either he will die or he will go down into battle and perish. Jehovah forbid that I should put forth my hand against Jehovah's anointed: but now take, I pray thee, the spear that is at his head and the cruse of water, and let us go."

And David took the spear and the cruse of water, and the two went away, and no one saw or knew that any one had been around the camp, for they were all sound asleep.

David went away across to a mountain-top and stood up and called to the people in King Saul's camp. The king's bodyguard answered David. His name was Abner, and he said, "Who are you that cries to the king?"

David called to Abner: "Art not thou a valiant man? Who is like to thee in Israel? Wherefore then hast thou not kept watch over thy lord, the king? for there came one of the people in to destroy the king."

Then David told Abner that he was not fit to live because he had not kept watch over his king. He added: "See where the king's spear is and the cruse of water that was at his head."

King Saul heard David's voice; always when King Saul was in the right kind of mood he loved to hear that voice, and now it seemed to soften all the anger against David. He knew that David had spared his life, and he said, "Is this thy voice, my son David?" And David answered, "It is my voice, O lord, my king."

Then King Saul called to David: "I have sinned: return, my son David; for I will no more do thee harm, because my life was precious in thine eyes this day: behold, I have played the fool."

David was not to be coaxed into the king's palace any more. He just called to the king: "Behold the spear, O king; let one of the young men come over and fetch it." Then he told King Saul that he had made up his mind to put his life into the hands of God. David said: "I am trusting my life in His hands." And Saul called to David, "Blessed be thou, my son David," and he returned to his palace and his men to their homes, and David, with his small group of men, went away to their own homes.

THE TWENTY-FOURTH PSALM

The
earth is Je-
hovah's and the
fulness thereof;
The world, and they that
dwell therein.
For He hath founded it upon
the seas,
And established it upon the floods.
Who shall ascend into the hill of Jehovah?
And who shall stand in His holy place?
He that hath clean hands, and a pure heart;
Who hath not lifted up his soul unto falsehood,
And hath not sworn deceitfully.
He shall receive a blessing from Jehovah.

· · · · · · · · · · · · · · · ·

Lift up your heads, O ye gates;
And be ye lifted up, ye everlasting doors:
And the King of glory will come in.
Who is the King of glory?

Jehovah strong and mighty,
Jehovah mighty in battle.
Lift up your heads, O ye gates;
Yea, lift them up, ye everlasting doors:
And the King of glory will come in.
Who is this King of glory?
Jehovah of hosts,
He is the King of glory.

93

ESTHER, THE BRAVE QUEEN

Many, many years ago there lived a king of
Persia whose name was Xerxes. He was
a son of King Darius, one of the most
powerful kings that ever reigned in
Persia.

King Xerxes wanted a new queen to reign
with him, and upon the advice of his no-
bles the most beautiful girls of his kingdom were invited to come before him.

There were some Jewish people who had lived
in Persia for many years, and one of
these Jews was a man named Mordecai.
Mordecai had been such a noble charac-
ter among them that he had been honored in the kingdom by being appointed
one of the king's officers.

Mordecai had a beautiful young cousin,

Esther, who lived in his home. She, too, belonged to the Jewish race, but Mordecai thought it would be fine if she might go before King Xerxes with all the other beautiful girls.

Esther very timidly went to the king's palace, and she saw a great many lovely maidens there. They wore such beautiful clothing, and jewels sparkled on their arms and fingers. Esther thought to herself, "The king will never choose me."

But when King Xerxes looked at Esther, when he heard her sweet, low voice and saw how gentle her manners were, he chose her to be the queen. She was surprised, and, of course, Mordecai was pleased.

There was a man in the king's court whose name was Haman. Haman was a very great man indeed, and he had been set over all the princes. Whenever Haman would go through the streets the people would bow before him, and this would please him very greatly. But there was one man in the kingdom who would not bow before Haman; that man was Mordecai, the Jew. And it made Haman very angry whenever he noticed that Mordecai would not bow to him.

Haman vowed that he would have vengeance on any man who would treat him that way. He knew that Mordecai was a Jew, but he did not know anything at all about the new queen, Esther. He made up his mind to ask the king to put an end to the Jews in the kingdom.

On the next day, when Haman stood before King Xerxes, he said: "O king, scattered abroad throughout your kingdom is a race of people who refuse to obey your laws; this ought not to be allowed, and you should make a decree that they should all be destroyed."

And the king immediately made the decree. This pleased Haman very much, because now he saw the end of the man Mordecai, who would not be his subject.

The matter was fixed up and the decree went forth that on the thirteenth day of the twelfth month all the Jews throughout the kingdom, men, women and children, should be put to death.

When Mordecai knew what was done, he rent his clothes and put sackcloth and ashes upon himself to signify his sore distress. The other Jews did the same thing. There was weeping and wailing.

Esther saw her cousin as he came to the king's gate, and she sent a servant to ask him what was the matter. When the servant went before Mordecai, the old man told him what had happened, and gave him a paper which would tell Queen Esther just what Haman had done. Then Mordecai said: "You take this to Queen Esther and tell her that she must go to the king and request him to save her people."

Queen Esther sent this message back to her cousin: "Every one in the kingdom knows that whoever shall come into the king's court unless he be called, shall be put to death, except those to whom the king shall hold out his golden scepter. I have not been called for thirty days." When this message reached Mordecai he im-

mediately sent word back to Esther not
to care for herself, because if all the Jews
were put to death she would certainly
perish with them.

Then the brave young queen thought about
all her people. She made up her mind
very quickly what she would do. She
told the servant to go back and tell Mordecai to call all the Jews of the city
together so that they might fast and
pray for her. She said: "Have them
neither eat nor drink for three days,
night nor day. I also and my maidens
will fast in like manner, and so will I
go in unto the king, which is not accord-
ing to the law: and if I perish, I perish."

Mordecai did the thing which Esther asked
him to do, and on the third day, while
the people were still fasting and praying,

Esther put on her royal robes, went into the inner court of the king's house and stood where the king might see her.

As he saw her standing there so beautiful before him, his heart was touched. He knew that she would not risk her life for any little thing, and so he held out the golden scepter. Then he said: "Queen Esther, what wilt thou? What is thy request? It shall be given thee to the half of my kingdom."

Then the queen asked him if he would come to a banquet which she had prepared for him. She asked also that Haman should come.

The king was pleased to go to the banquet, and so was the wicked Haman. At the banquet the queen told the king what had happened. She told him that she belonged to the race of people who were to be put to death, and she begged him to spare them.

When the king heard that his royal, beautiful queen was a Jewess, and that he himself had signed the decree that they should be killed, he was very angry and caused the wicked Haman to be hanged on the very gallows that Haman had built for Mordecai. And Esther's bravery was rewarded.

THANKSGIVING

Sangster.

Lillien Helburn.

1. For peace and for plen - ty, for free - dom, for rest, For
2. For wak - ing and sleep - ing, for bless - ings to be, We

joy in the land from the east to the west, For the
chil - dren would of - fer our prais - es to Thee; For

dear star - ry flag with its red, white and blue, We
God is our Fath - er, and bends from a - bove, To

thank Thee from hearts that are hon - est and true.
keep the round world in the smile of His love.

THREE HEROES

No doubt you remember the story of Daniel and his three companions, Hananiah, Mishael and Azariah, as they were taken into the king's palace when they refused to drink the king's wine or eat the rich food that the steward brought.

King Nebuchadnezzar soon learned to love these young men, and to want them to stay in his service. They were his officers for a great many years, and then something happened which proved these three men were very brave.

These young men, like Daniel, had been taught never to do anything which was wrong, but they were faithful to their king, doing all the things which he required of them.

Although Nebuchadnezzar was a heathen, and did not know or believe in Daniel's God, he was very kind and would do anything in his power for these men.

In King Nebuchadnezzar's country the people all worshiped idols, and once a very hard test came to our three heroes, Hananiah, Mishael and Azariah.

Nebuchadnezzar thought because he was such a powerful king that he ought to build a huge, golden idol for his people, larger and finer than any idols that had ever been built. At last it was finished, and there it stood, a great, fine idol, built of gold, ninety feet high, worth millions of dollars.

The king was very proud of this idol, and the time came when he wanted to dedicate it. He sent out to all the rulers and captains and officers of his kingdom and told them to come to a place called Dura, which was just outside the city of Babylon. The idol had been placed there, and there was to be a great celebration as the people looked upon it and worshiped it for the first time. There were to be bands of music, and Nebuchadnezzar commanded that when the people heard the music on the flute, the cornet, harp and other instruments they should fall down and worship the idol.

Among the officers and governors were Hananiah, Mishael and Azariah. They had made up their minds what they were going to do; they knew that the king wanted very much for every one of his subjects to bow to the idol; they knew that the King in heaven had commanded them never to bow down to an idol. King Nebuchadnezzar had said: "If there should be any one that will not fall down and worship this idol, he shall be cast into a fiery furnace."

What should these three men do? They knew what would happen to them if they did not bow down before this image, and they knew also that they would be untrue to God if they did fall down before it.

What do you think these Hebrews who had always been so strong and brave did? Listen; when the sound of the music was heard, everybody fell down to the earth and worshiped the golden idol—all but these three.

Some of the people told Nebuchadnezzar. They said: "There are some Hebrews who did not fall down to worship the golden image." Oh, but the king was angry! He was angry because anybody in that whole country dared to disobey him, and he sent for the three men to be brought to him. The king decided to give them one more chance. He said: "Now, if you are ready, at the sound of the music, to fall down before the image which I have made, well: but if you do not, you shall be cast into the midst of a burning, fiery furnace, and who is that God who shall deliver you out of my hand?"

The men answered and said: "O Nebuchadnezzar, if you do this, our God whom we serve, he is able to deliver us from the burning, fiery furnace, and he will deliver us out of thy hand, O king." Then they said to the angry king: "We will not serve thy gods, nor worship the golden image which thou hast set up."

Then the king was very angry indeed, and he commanded his men to heat the furnace ever so much hotter than it had ever been before. He said: "Heat it seven times hotter than you always do." The king called others of his strong men and told them to bind these three who had disobeyed him and throw them into the furnace.

The king's servants took Hananiah, Mishael and Azariah and bound them. They left all the clothes on the men, but bound them so they could not move hand or foot, and they took them and threw them into the midst of the furnace.

King Nebuchadnezzar was watching all this time, and when he looked into the furnace, instead of three men, he saw four, and they were not bound at all. They were standing there free in the furnace, and the fire was not hurting them one bit. They were not burned; they were not even scorched. Nebuchadnezzar was so astonished he did not know what to do. He said to his servants, "Did not we cast three men into the furnace?" and they answered, "We did." Then he said: "I see four men walking in the midst of the fire, and they are not hurt. They are the three Hebrews, and there is one other like unto a son of the gods." God had sent His angel to be with the three men who were standing for what was right. Are you wondering what King Nebuchadnezzar did? Well, he just walked to the mouth of the furnace and

called to the three Hebrew children to come out.

Then Hananiah, Mishael and Azariah came out of the fire, and the people who were standing there could not tell that they had been in the fire; they were alive and well and strong; they were not burned at all, and there was not even the smell of fire about their clothes.

It was God's great power that had saved them, and King Nebuchadnezzar sent out word that no one in all his country should speak a word against the God of these three men, he said, "For there is no other god able to deliver after this sort."

AMERICA

My country! 'tis of thee,
Sweet land of liberty,
  Of thee I sing;
Land where my fathers died,
Land of the pilgrims' pride,
From every mountainside
  Let freedom ring!

My native country, thee,
Land of the noble, free,
  Thy name I love;
I love thy rocks and rills,
Thy woods and templed hills;
My heart with rapture thrills,
  Like that above.

Let music swell the breeze,
And ring from all the trees
  Sweet freedom's song;
Let mortal tongues awake;
Let all that breathe partake;
Let rocks their silence break,
  The sound prolong.

Our fathers' God! to Thee,
Author of liberty,
  To Thee we sing;
Long may our land be bright
With freedom's holy light;
Protect us by Thy might,
  Great God, our King!

                              —*S. F. Smith.*

DANIEL THE FEARLESS

Perhaps there never was a more fearless man than Daniel. It may have been because he was always careful to do the right. He knew he was doing right when he obeyed the law of God, and this made him fearless.

As a Jewish lad Daniel had been taken prisoner by some soldiers and carried with hundreds of other prisoners into a distant country. He, with three companions, who were likewise full of courage, were chosen to become the king's helpers. And it came to pass as the years went by that the king knew he could trust Daniel with anything.

A powerful king, named Nebuchadnezzar, ruled in Babylon, and he grew very fond of Daniel, for the reason that Daniel had been able to do some things which no one else could do.

King Nebuchadnezzar had had a very strange dream, and when he wakened in the morning he could not recall it; still, the thing troubled him, and he called for his wise men and magicians to come to the palace and tell him its meaning. He required that the one who came must not only tell him the meaning of the dream, but tell him what the dream itself was.

Magicians, enchanters and sorcerers were brought before him, and they told the king that if he would tell them what the dream was they would tell its meaning; but King Nebuchadnezzar was helpless because he could not remember what the dream had been. However, he grew very angry at the men and ordered that all the wise men of the kingdom should be slain.

The captain of the king's guard was hunting for Daniel that he might be slain also. Then Daniel asked why the rule had been made that all the wise men should be slain, and the captain told him the story of the king's dream.

Daniel wished that he might try to tell the king what the dream meant, and yet he did not know what the dream had been. He went home to the three friends who had been taken captive with him and had served in the king's palace all these years with him. Daniel told them the story and said to them: "Pray that God will give us the secret of this dream." And that night God gave Daniel the

power to tell what the dream was and what it meant.

Daniel said: "I thank thee and praise thee, O thou God of my fathers, who has given me wisdom and might, and has now made known unto me what we desire of thee."

Then Daniel went before the king and told him the meaning. He saved the lives of all the wise men and magicians, and the very fact that he could tell the dream and its meaning made the king love and trust him more.

Later the king had another dream and called for Daniel. This time Daniel was very sorry to interpret the dream, because it meant that the king's crown was to be taken away from him. And, after awhile, the thing came to pass just as Daniel said it would.

Now, a new king, whose name was Belshazzar, came to the throne of Babylon; he was a reckless sort of man who did not care for anything but his own pleasure and greatness.

One evening King Belshazzar was giving a great feast. A thousand of his lords were at the feast, and the king became so excited after he had used a great deal of wine that he thought he would do something very daring. He commanded his servants to bring in the gold and silver vessels which had been stolen from the house of God in Jerusalem, and began to drink wine from them.

While they drank the wine they praised the gods of gold and of silver, of brass and of iron, of wood and of stone. And while they were doing this a very strange thing happened. The fingers of a hand came out and wrote against the plaster of the wall of the king's palace, and the king saw part of the hand that wrote. The king was so frightened that his knees began to shake, and he cried out that the enchanters and sorcerers should be brought in.

He promised that the one who would tell him what the writing meant should be clothed with purple and have a gold chain put about his neck, and that he should become the third ruler in the kingdom.

Many wise men came, but they could not tell the king what the handwriting was. At last the queen came into the banquet-room. She said: "O king, live forever; let not thy thoughts trouble thee. There is a man in thy kingdom in whom is the spirit of the holy gods." Then the queen went on to tell him of the goodness and nobleness of the man Daniel. She told him how Daniel had interpreted the dreams of Nebuchadnezzar. Then she said: "Now let Daniel be called, and he will show thee the interpretation."

The king sent for Daniel, and when he came into the court the king spoke to him: "Art thou that Daniel who art of the children of Judah, whom the king, my father, brought out of Judah?"

Then King Belshazzar told Daniel that he had heard much of him, and told him about the writing on the wall. Then he said: "Now, if thou canst read the writing and make known to me its meaning, thou shalt be clothed with purple and have a chain of gold about thy neck, and

shalt be the third ruler in the kingdom."
Daniel said: "Let thy gifts be to thyself, O
king, and give thy rewards to another;
nevertheless, I will read the writing unto
the king and make known its meaning."
Then Daniel read these strange words:
"Mene, mene, tekel, upharsin." He told
the king that the first word, MENE,
meant "God hath numbered thy kingdom and brought it to an end." Then
Daniel said, "The third word, TEKEL,
means thou art weighed in the bal-
ances and art found wanting." "And
the last word means, Thy kingdom is
divided and given to the Medes and Per-
sians."
King Belshazzar was as good as his word.
He commanded that Daniel should be
clothed with purple, that a chain of gold

be put about his neck, and that he become the third ruler in the kingdom.

That night King Belshazzar was slain, and the very things which Daniel had spoken of came to pass. It had not been easy for Daniel to stand before the great king and tell him that his kingdom was to be taken away from him. It had taken a great deal of courage to do this, but Daniel was ever ready to do right things even though they were hard.

"Dare to be a Daniel,
Dare to stand alone;
Dare to have a purpose firm,
Dare to make it known."

DARE TO DO RIGHT

Bradbury.

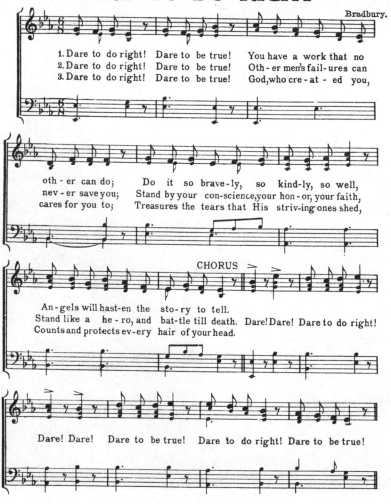

1. Dare to do right! Dare to be true! You have a work that no oth - er can do; Do it so brave-ly, so kind-ly, so well, An - gels will hast-en the sto - ry to tell.

2. Dare to do right! Dare to be true! Oth - er men's fail - ures can nev - er save you; Stand by your con-science, your hon - or, your faith, Stand like a he - ro, and bat-tle till death.

3. Dare to do right! Dare to be true! God, who cre - at - ed you, cares for you to; Treasures the tears that His striv-ing ones shed, Counts and protects ev-ery hair of your head.

CHORUS

Dare! Dare! Dare to do right! Dare! Dare! Dare to be true! Dare to do right! Dare to be true!

ON GUARD

(Poem over six hundred years old.)

Guard, my child, thy tongue,
That it speak no wrong:
Let no evil word pass o'er it;
Set the watch of truth before it,
That it speak no wrong;
Guard, my child, thy tongue.

Guard, my child, thine eyes;
Prying is not wise:
Let them look on what is right,
From all evil turn their sight.
Prying is not wise:
Guard, my child, thine eyes.

Guard, my child, thine ear;
Wicked words will sear:
Let no evil word come in,
That may cause thy soul to sin;
Wicked words will sear:
Guard, my child, thine ear.

ELIJAH

Often in the olden time God spoke to the people who loved and served Him. Most of the time He sent His messages through one man; this man was usually a prophet. There was one prophet whose name was Elijah, that carried God's messages to the people for nearly eighteen years, and many times it was not an easy thing to do. Many times Elijah's life was threatened, but he always did what God asked of him, and the Father in heaven always took care of him.

One time when a wicked, wicked king was the ruler of the people of Israel, God told Elijah to go to this King Ahab and tell him that there should be no rain nor dew until He saw fit to send it.

King Ahab and all the people were very angry at Elijah when this message came, but God was caring for His servant; he told Elijah just where to hide, by a brook where there was plenty of water, and He said, "I have commanded the ravens to feed thee there." Every morning and evening for many, many days, the ravens brought Elijah bread and meat, and after the brook dried up God directed Elijah just where to go that he might obtain food and water.

Elijah was cared for in this way for a long, long time. Nearly three years had passed when one day God said to him: "Go, show thyself unto Ahab, and I will send rain upon the earth."

Elijah knew that Ahab had the most wicked wife in all the world; she was a heathen woman whose name was Jezebel, and Ahab had himself begun to worship idols after she came to live at his home.

When Elijah was on his way to see Ahab he met one of his old friends, another prophet, and this prophet begged Elijah not to go to Ahab, for he was afraid that Jezebel would kill them both, but Elijah said: "As Jehovah of hosts liveth, before whom I stand, I will surely show myself unto him to-day."

When King Ahab heard that Elijah was coming, he went out to meet him and said to him, "Is it thou, thou troubler of Israel?"

Elijah answered, "I have not troubled Israel." Then Elijah told Ahab of his own faults, and planned a great contest, when he himself, as God's prophet, should meet with all the prophets of the heathen god,

Baal, to decide which was the true God.

Elijah said to Ahab: "You send all the prophets of Baal to Mount Carmel, and I will meet them there."

King Ahab was so sure the prophets of Baal could do something that he sent and brought them all together, and more than four hundred other prophets that were false also. They all came to Mount Carmel.

Mount Carmel is a great, long ridge about twelve miles in length, and one side of it is sloping, while the other side is very steep and dangerous.

Elijah was not one bit afraid to meet all the people of Israel and the prophets upon the mountainside. He stepped out in front of them and told them about the trial they were going to make. He told them that each should get his offering ready, and that first he would give them a trial. They should call on their god to send down fire to burn the offering. When the offering was on the altar these people began praying and calling, "Oh, Baal, hear us," but there was no answer, and some of the prophets leaped about the altar and cried louder, "Oh, Baal, hear us."

Elijah stood back and looked at them. He said: "Why don't you cry louder? maybe he is gone to sleep; you had better waken him up; maybe he has gone on a journey." The people were so frantic they cried still louder. All day long they cried to their god Baal, but no answer came. Then in the evening Elijah fixed up his altar. He took the greatest care in fixing it up.

After the offering was cut up and laid on the altar, he had some people fill jars with water and pour it on the wood. Then he told them to put more water on, and more; and then it began to run down and around the ditch.

Then Elijah stepped out and prayed to God in the quietest kind of way: "O Jehovah, the God of Abraham and of Isaac and of Jacob, let it be known in Israel this day that thou art God in Israel, and that I am thy servant. Hear me, O Jehovah, hear me, that the people may know that thou art God and that thou hast turned their hearts back again."

Immediately the fire came down and burned up the offering. It burned even the stones and water. Then the people shouted, "Jehovah is God, Jehovah is God."

It was God's plan that these prophets of Baal should be put to death, and they were thrown over the steep precipice, on the side of Mount Carmel.

Then King Ahab went home and told the wicked Jezebel what had happened to the prophets. She was so angry with Elijah that she declared she would take his life before another day.

Elijah was frightened at Jezebel's word, and he started away to a far part of the country. After awhile he sat down to rest under a tree. Then he fell asleep and God sent an angel to feed him there. At his head lay a cake baked on coals and a cruse of water was there also. Elijah heard a voice say, "Arise and eat," and after he had eaten he lay down again and went to sleep.

After he had slept a little while the angel of
God came again and told him to arise and
eat, because he was to go on a long trip.
This made Elijah wonder, and perhaps
you will think that it frightened him
when God said to him, "Go, return."
Was Elijah to return to the wicked King
Ahab? Was he to go back to the country where the queen would surely be
watching to put him to death?
Then God told Elijah that he should anoint
another man to be king over Israel in
place of the wicked King Ahab. He told
him also that he should anoint a new
prophet to take his place. This prophet
should be Elisha.
Then, one day, after this had all been done,
Elijah and Elisha walked together; they
came up to the river Jordan, and, some-

how, Elijah knew that he was about to go away from the earth. He said to Elisha: "Is there anything you would like to have me do for you?" And the young man said: "Only help me to be as good as you have been." Elijah answered: "You have asked a hard thing, something that I can not do myself, but God will make a sign to you that if you see me when I am taken from you, it shall be so; if you do not see me, it shall not be so." As they went out the most beautiful thing happened to Elijah. A great, brilliant light shone in the sky—a chariot of fire —and Elijah was caught up by a great whirlwind into heaven. When Elisha saw Elijah going up he cried, "My father, my father," and then he went out to do the work as nearly like Elijah as he could.

O LITTLE TOWN OF BETHLEHEM

O little town of Bethlehem,
How still we see thee lie!
Above thy deep and dreamless sleep
The silent stars go by:
Yet in thy dark streets shineth
The everlasting Light;
The hopes and fears of all the years
Are met in thee to-night.

For Christ is born of Mary;
And, gathered all above,
While mortals sleep, the angels keep
Their watch of wondering love.
O morning stars, together
Proclaim the holy birth;
And praises sing to God the King,
And peace to men on earth.

How silently, how silently,
    The wondrous gift is given;
So God imparts to human hearts
    The blessings of His heaven.
No ear may hear His coming,
    But in this world of sin,
Where meek souls will receive Him still,
    The dear Christ enters in.

O holy Child of Bethlehem,
    Descend to us, we pray;
Cast out our sin, and enter in;
    Be born in us to-day.
We hear the Christmas angels
    The great, glad tidings tell;
O come to us, abide with us,
    Our Lord Emmanuel!

—Phillips Brooks.

CHRISTMAS

"In another land and time,
Long ago and far away,
Was a little baby born
On the first glad Christmas Day.

"Words of truth and deeds of love
Filled His life from day to day,
So that all the world was blest
On the first glad Christmas Day.

"Little children did He love
With a tender love alway;
So should little children be
Always glad on Christmas Day."

I Heard the Bells On Christmas Day.

Henry W. Longfellow.

J. Baptiste Calkin.

1. I heard the bells on Christ-mas Day Their old fam - il - iar car - ols play,
2. I thought how, as the day had come, The bel-fries of all Chris - ten-dom
3. Till ring - ing, sing - ing on its way, The world revolved from night to day,
4. And in de - spair I bowed my head: "There is no peace on earth," I said,
5. Then pealed the bells more loud and deep: "God is not dead, nor doth He sleep;

And wild and sweet the words re - peat Of peace on earth, good-will to men.
Had rolled a - long th' un-bro - ken song Of peace on earth, good-will to men.
A voice, a chime, a chant sub-lime, Of peace on earth, good-will to men.
"For hate is strong and mocks the song Of peace on earth, good-will to men."
The wrong shall fail, the right pre - vail, With peace on earth, good-will to men."

JESUS

In a country far beyond the sea is a city called Nazareth, and two good people, Mary and Joseph, lived there. The king of that country sent a message that all the people must go to the city of Bethlehem to have their names enrolled.

Joseph was a good man who always obeyed his king's commands, and he and Mary started on the long trip. Mary rode on a donkey, and her husband walked beside her.

When they reached the city of Bethlehem it was full of people who had come on the same errand as themselves, and when they went to the hotel the innkeeper told them that he had no room for them. At last they found a place to sleep.

Perhaps you will think it was not a very nice place, because all the rooms in all the homes were taken and there was nothing left but a place in the stable. However, the stable was nice and clean.

In the night-time the baby Jesus was born, and Mary placed Him in the manger with straw for a bed.

It did not take very long for the news of Jesus' coming to spread over the little city. God Himself told the people that His Son had come to earth. Away out on the hillside shepherds were watching their flocks by night, and all at once an angel appeared before them, the glory of God shone round about them, and the angel said to them: "Be not afraid; for, behold, I bring you good tidings of great joy which shall be to all people; for there

is born to you this day in the city of
David a Saviour, who is Christ the Lord.
And this is the sign unto you; ye shall
find the babe wrapped in swaddling
clothes and lying in a manger."
Just as the angel finished speaking, a great
multitude of angels filled the sky and
sang:
"Glory to God in the highest,
And on earth peace, good will toward men."

Then the shepherds went to find Jesus. They
fell down and worshiped Him and returned to their work on the hillside.

Some little time after this, Wise-men came
from the far east; they, too, came to worship, and they brought the richest gifts
which they could find in their country,
for they knew that they were worshiping
a new king.

With the coming of the Wise-men, Jesus'
troubles began. Wicked King Herod

was not pleased when he heard from these Wise-men that a new king had been born, for he supposed that it was some one come to take his earthly kingdom from him, and he began at that time to make trouble. He asked the Wise-men all the questions that he possibly could, and tried to find out just where the baby was, so that he could send officers to take Jesus' life. But God was caring for His Son. He caused a dream to come to the Wise-men in which they were warned not to go back to Herod's palace, but to go home another way, and this they did. Jesus grew and grew, as babies always do, and He learned beautiful lessons from his mother, Mary. He spent many hours around the little carpenter shop in Nazareth with Joseph, and helped in any way that a small child could. It would just be wonderful if we could tell the beautiful things that happened at that little home. We are just sure that Jesus played a great deal; we are sure that He listened to the birds' songs, and that He saw the wild flowers and all the beautiful things that were around Him. And we are certain that Mary and Joseph were blessed in having Him with them.

One day He went to the temple, and He was just old enough to be thinking very deeply about the things which He saw, and the things which He heard the learned men teaching. So He spent quite a bit of His time talking to these doctors in the temple. At last He became lost from Mary and Joseph, and it took three whole days to find Him, and when they finally did, there He was in the temple, talking with learned doctors and wise men.

After His mother spoke to Him, very quietly He left the men and went home to Nazareth, and there He worked with Joseph and grew to manhood.

At last we find Him ready to go about the business for which He was sent—that of helping people to be true to God.

And now begins a life full of helpfulness and courage and hurts and stings. You would not think that any one would want to hurt the feelings of Jesus, and yet from the time that He began to cure people of their diseases and to help them in all the ways which they needed, some people were always ready to nag at Him and to say ugly things about Him.

But He never minded these things; He went about making the blind eyes to see, lame legs to walk, deaf ears to hear, dumb tongues to speak—healing all manner of diseases and helping all those who were in distress until His own body was weary.

He knew that He would not stay a very great many years upon the earth, and that the work which He had started must be carried on by others, so He called around Him a group of helpers, twelve of them; men staunch and true; men whom He had found faithfully doing their little tasks in life. There was one whose name was Peter; another, John, and these were always close by the Master's side.

But there were those who were always questioning and watching; those who were always trying to get something against

Him. They wanted Him out of the way, and there was no honest way to do this, and they just demanded of the rulers that He be put to death.

One evening when Jesus had been with His group of very close friends He let them understand that He knew that very soon this would happen to Him.

You would not think that one of the close friends of Jesus would ever say anything against Him, but there was one man who was tempted when somebody offered him money if he would give Jesus into their hands. And on the same evening when Jesus had told them all the things that would happen to Him, Judas Iscariot slipped away from the supper-table and went out to the chief officers and told them where they would be likely to find Jesus. He knew where Jesus would probably go as soon as the supper was over, and he had arranged that a great crowd of people should go with him, and he would point Jesus out to them. He said to them: "Whomsoever I shall kiss, that is he; take him."

When the crowd came up, Judas spoke to Jesus and said, "Hail, Rabbi." Then he walked up and kissed Jesus. Immediately the officers in the mob laid hands on Jesus and took Him.

They took Jesus away to the house of a man by the name of Caiaphas, the high priest, and His disciples followed along, not knowing what to do.

All the chief priests and the council tried to find witnesses who would make false charges against Jesus, but they did not find any. Later there were two that were found who made charges which these officers called "blasphemy."

They treated the kind, loving Saviour in the most terrible way that night. The Bible tells us that "then did they spit in his face and buffet him: and some smote him with the palms of their hands." Then they mocked Him and said: "Prophesy unto us, thou Christ. Who is it that struck thee?"

After awhile they decided that Jesus should go before the governor, Pilate. And this man could find no fault in Jesus at all. Pilate tried every way to get them to have Jesus released, but the mob would not do it. They yelled and cried out: "If thou lettest this man go, thou art not Cæsar's friend." They said that to make

159

Pilate afraid of the great king, Cæsar. That was their way of telling Pilate that if he did not do something they would see that he lost his office.

When Pilate grew afraid of losing his office he just released Jesus to the mob, and they took him out to the hillside, and, amid all kinds of abuse and scorn and mockery, He was placed on the cross.

But Jesus did not revile those who abused Him; as He hung upon the cross He cried to the Father in heaven: "Father, forgive them, they know not what they do." And with that spirit of love and kindness to all, He died.

A great darkness came over the earth for three long hours, and many of the people were frightened and began to wish that they had not treated Jesus so badly.

After Jesus had died a man by the name of
Joseph came and begged that he might
put the body in his own tomb. The ruler
did not care, and Joseph, with some
others to help him, took the body from
the cross and placed it in the tomb.
After the body was placed in the tomb the
officers began to think that maybe Jesus'
friends might come and take His body
away, and they placed a guard of soldiers on each side of the door.
Very early on Sunday morning Mary Magdalene and the other Mary went to the place
where Jesus had been laid, and when
they reached the tomb the stone had been
rolled away. An angel was sitting inside.
He said to the women: "Fear not ye; he
is not here, for he is risen. Come and
see the place where the Lord lay."

A little later the women saw Jesus and He
gave them a message which He wanted
them to carry to His very dear friends.
After this He saw His friends only a few
times.

One day, when all of them were present, they
walked out on the hillside together, and,
after giving them beautiful words of
helpfulness, Jesus lifted His hands toward heaven and went to be with the
Father there.

PETER, THE FISHERMAN

Among the very close friends of Jesus was
one man whose name was Simon Peter.
The lakeshore of Galilee is thickly dotted
with cities and villages, and many of the
people from these earned their living by
catching fish and selling them.
Simon Peter was a man who earned his living
in this way. He and his brother Andrew
were partners in this business. James
and John, two other of Jesus' close
friends, were partners also.
One day when Jesus was selecting the helpers with whom he wanted to leave His
work on earth, He came across Peter.
Jesus watched Peter for awhile, and there was
something about him that made Jesus
feel that he would be an honest, faithful

man in His work, so He called him to be one of His disciples. From that time on to the crucifixion Peter was with Jesus a very great deal.

When Jesus preached the great Sermon on the Mount, Peter was among those who listened. Jesus taught him how to pray, how to forgive and how to be helpful. Jesus very often visited in Peter's home, and ate at his table, and so the two were very, very good friends.

One day when Jesus went to this home He found Peter's wife's mother very sick in bed. He took the old lady by the hand and she sat up strong and well.

Many times Peter saw Jesus when He made sick people well or helped the blind to see and the lame to walk, and each time that he saw, it made him glad that Jesus had chosen him to be a friend and helper. He stayed very close to the kind Teacher until one day when he was all worried and beside himself; that was the time when Jesus' enemies were clamoring for His life; they wanted Him to be crucified.

Just a little while before this Peter had told Jesus that he would always stay close to Him, and Jesus had answered, "Before the cock shall crow you will deny me thrice." Peter's answer to Him had been, "Even if I must die with thee, yet I will not deny thee."

Peter was so in earnest when he said this that nobody could have doubted his word, but that night, somehow, in some way, he did deny that he knew Jesus, and even when the question was asked of him the third time he answered, "I know not the man." At that moment Peter heard a cock crow and looked up; Jesus had turned and was looking right at him. It was not until that moment that Peter remembered himself; then he went out and wept bitterly. His sorrow was very great. He had denied his Lord!

After Jesus' resurrection Peter was among the group which met Him; he was anxious to get very close to Jesus, perhaps to tell Him how sorry he had been. Jesus, however, knew this already, and one day, down close to the seaside, when Peter and the others had been fishing, and after they had had their breakfast together, Jesus turned to Peter and said, "Lovest thou me?" And Peter was glad to answer, "Lord, thou knowest I love thee." Jesus asked him a second time, and Peter answered in the same way; even a third time did Jesus ask the question, "Simon, son of John, lovest thou me?" Peter was just a little grieved that Jesus should ask him the same question three times, but perhaps it was because there had been three times when he denied Jesus.

It was not long after this that Jesus ascended to heaven, and Peter and John

and the others were left to carry on His
work here on the earth.

Peter had been a coward at one time, but
never again. He went out in Jesus' name
doing whatever he could to help people.
He and John traveled around and did
many wonderful works through the power
that came from heaven.

One time Peter was thrown into prison, and
the king intended to bring him out and
kill him just to please the people, not because he had done anything wrong; but
at this time there was a great feast going
on and the king dare not kill anybody
then, because that would be unlawful.

While Peter was in prison his friends met
together in the home of a woman named
Mary to pray for him.

They knew that the king would doubtless put

171

him to death, and these people prayed
and prayed that this should not happen.
It was such a wonderful prayer-meeting,
lasting many days and nights, but these
people knew that God was the only one
who could save Peter from the cruel
king.
On the last day of the feast the people were
still praying, and in the dark prison-room
all at once something happened. There
were two soldiers guarding the door,
one on either side, and on the inside
Peter was chained to two soldiers; but
all at once a bright light shone in the
prison-room and there was an angel who
touched Peter on the side and said:
"Arise quickly, Peter; put on your san-
dals and your garments and follow me."
And he led Peter right out of the room

and down to the home where the prayer-meeting was being held.

The people there were very much surprised when Peter came walking in, but they knew that it was God's power that had saved him.

One day there was a man who had been lame all his life sitting at the Beautiful Gate of the temple. He was begging from the people who came past him. When Peter and John came by they saw the beggar. Peter said: "Silver and gold have I none, but what I have that I give thee. In the name of Jesus Christ of Nazareth, walk." He took the lame man by the hand, and immediately the feet and ankle-bones received strength and the man leaped up and stood and began to walk.

Then there arose a great questioning among

the people, and Peter preached to them a very wonderful sermon, so wonderful that the people marveled. They said, "Why, Peter and John are unlearned, ignorant men." And the people could say nothing in answer to the words which Peter spoke.

Peter never felt that he had honored Jesus in the way that he should; he never felt that he had made up for having denied his Lord and Master three times on that dreadful night, but he served Jesus truly. He was a brave, valiant hero, doing his Master's bidding up until the very day of his death. Many times he was beaten, many times he was illtreated for the sake of Jesus' name, but the kind Master only loved him the more for standing this abuse without complaint.

LIST OF BIBLICAL WORDS

For convenience, we append this table of Biblical names. Authority for pronunciation is the new American Standard Revised Version of the Bible.

Abishai—a-bĭsh′a-i.
Abner—ăb′ner.
Abraham—ā′bra-ham.
Agrippa—a-grĭp′pa.
Ahab—ā′hăb.
Azariah—ăz′a-rī′ah.

Baal—bā′al.
Babylon—băb′y-lon.
Belshazzar—bel-shăz′zar.
Benjamin—bĕn′ja-min.
Bethlehem—bĕth′-le-hem.

Cæsar—çæ′şar.
Cæsarea—çæş′a-rē′a.
Caiaphas—eā′ia-phas.
Canaan—eā′naan.
Carmel—eär′mel.
Chilion—ehĭl′ĭ-on.
Cleopas—elē′o-päs.

Darius—da-rī′us.
Didymus—dĭd′y-mŭs.
Dura—dū′ra.

Egypt—ē′gypt.
Egyptian—ē-gyp′tian.
Elijah—e-lī′jah.
Elimelech—e-lĭm′e-leeh.
Elisha—e-lī′sha.
Emmaus—em-mā′us.
Esther—ĕs′ther.

Galilee—ğăl′i-lee.
Gentiles—ğĕn′tĭles.
Gerar—ğē′rär.
Gethsemane—ğeth-sĕm′a-ne.
Gideon—ğĭd′e-on.

Haman—hā′man.
Hananiah—hăn′a-nī′ah.
Hebrew—hē′brew.

Herod—hĕr′od.

Isaac—ī′saac.

Jehovah—je-hō′vah.
Jethro—jē′thro.
Jezebel—jĕz′e-bel.
Jordan—jôr′dan.
Judas Iscariot—jū′das is-eăr′i-ot.

Mahlon—mäh′lon.
Mary—mā′ry.
Magdalene—măg′da-lē′ne.
Midian—mĭd′i-an.
Midianite—mĭd′i-an-īte.
Mishael—mĭsh′a-el.
Moab—mō′ab.
Mordecai—môr′de-eai.
Moriah—mo-rī′ah.

Naomi—na-ō′mi.
Nazarene—năz′a-rēne.
Nazareth—năz′a-reth.
Nebo—nē′bo.
Nebuchadnezzar—nĕb′u-ehăd-nĕz′zar.
Nehemiah—nē′he-mī′ah.

Orpah—ôr′pah.

Persia—pĕr′si-a.
Pharaoh—phā′raōh.
Philistines—phĭ-lĭs′tĭnes.
Pilate—pī′late.
Potiphar—pŏt′i-phar.

Rabboni—răb-bō′nī.
Rebekah—rē-bĕk′âh.

Sheol—shē′ōl.

Xerxes—zĕrks′ĕş.

Zebedee—zĕb′e-dēe.

176